A Day in the Life: Polar Animals

Emperor Penguin

Katie Marsico

Heinemann Library
Chicago, Illinois

www.heinemannraintree.com
Visit our website to find out
more information about
Heinemann-Raintree books.

To order:

☎ Phone 888-454-2279

▭ Visit www.heinemannraintree.com
to browse our catalog and order online.

Edited by Rebecca Rissman, Daniel Nunn, and
Sian Smith
Designed by Joanna Hinton-Malivoire
Picture research by Hannah Taylor
Originated by Capstone Global Library Ltd
Printed in China

17 16 15 14
10 9 8 7 6

**Library of Congress Cataloging-in-
Publication Data**
Marsico, Katie, 1980-
    Emperor penguin / Katie Marsico.—1st ed.
      p. cm.—(A day in the life: polar animals)
    Includes bibliographical references and index.
    ISBN 978-1-4329-5327-0 (hc)
    ISBN 978-1-4329-5334-8 (pb)
    1. Emperor penguin—Juvenile literature. I. Title.
    QL696.S473M363 2012
    598.47—dc22   2010049854

Acknowledgments
We would like to thank the following for permission to
reproduce photographs: Corbis pp. 12 (Paul Nicklen),
14 (Ralph Lee Hopkins), 18 (Frans Lanting), 23d (Gerald
& Buff Corsi/Visuals Unlimited Inc.); Getty Images
pp. 9 (Minden Pictures/Pete Oxford), 13 (Nobert Wu);
Photolibrary pp. 7, 23f (Picture Press/Thorsten Milse), 8,
23b (Superstock/ John Higdon), 10, 23a (All Canada
Photos/ Wayne Lynch), 11 (Oxford Scientific/Doug Allan),
15 (Oxford Scientific/Oliver Kruger), 17 (Photononstop/
Christian Simonet), 19 (Tsuneo Nakamura), 20 (Peter
Arnold Images/Bruno P Zehnder), 22 (Oxford Scientific/
Sue Flood); Shutterstock pp. 4 (© Bryan Lintott), 5, 16, 21,
23c (© Gentoo Multimedia Ltd.), 6, 23e (© Armin Rose).

Cover photograph of emperor penguins (Aptenodytes
forsteri) near their nesting colony at Atka Bay, Weddell
Sea, Antarctica reproduced with permission of Photolibrary
(All Canada Photos/ Wayne Lynch). Back cover
photographs reproduced with permission of Shutterstock:
flipper (© Armin Rose), chick (© Gentoo Multimedia Ltd.).
The publisher would like to thank Michael Bright for his
assistance in the preparation of this book.

Every effort has been made to contact copyright holders
of material reproduced in this book. Any omissions will
be rectified in subsequent printings if notice is given to the
publisher.

Disclaimer
All the Internet addresses (URLs) given in this book were
valid at the time of going to press. However, due to the
dynamic nature of the Internet, some addresses may have
changed or ceased to exist since publication. While the
author and publishers regret any inconvenience this may
cause readers, no responsibility for any such changes can
be accepted by either the author or the publishers.

Contents

Some words are shown in bold, **like this**.
You can find them in the glossary on page 23.

What Is an Emperor Penguin?

An emperor penguin is a large bird that lives in snowy areas.

Birds are feathered animals that have wings and lay eggs.

Emperor penguins cannot fly.

They have other ways of surviving in a world of snow and ice.

What Do Emperor Penguins Look Like?

feathers

flipper

Emperor penguins are the largest type of penguin.

They are mainly black and white but have some yellow feathers.

These feathers are **waterproof** and keep the birds warm and dry.

Emperor penguins also have **webbed** feet and flippers to help them swim.

Where Do Emperor Penguins Live?

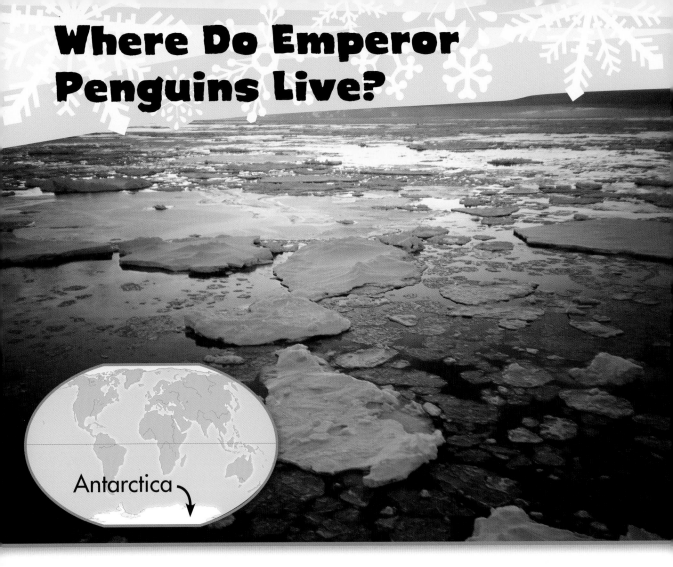

Antarctica

Emperor penguins live in **Antarctica**.

In Antarctica it is light all day and all night for part of the summer.

In Antarctica it is dark all day and all night for part of the winter.

Antarctica is the coldest and windiest place on Earth.

What Do Emperor Penguins Do in the Day?

Emperor penguins are usually most **active** during the day.

They spend the day swimming and searching for food.

Emperor penguins are excellent swimmers and divers.

They dive underwater for about two to eight minutes, before going up for air.

What Do Emperor Penguins Eat?

krill

Emperor penguins use their beaks to catch fish.

They also eat squid and tiny animals called **krill**.

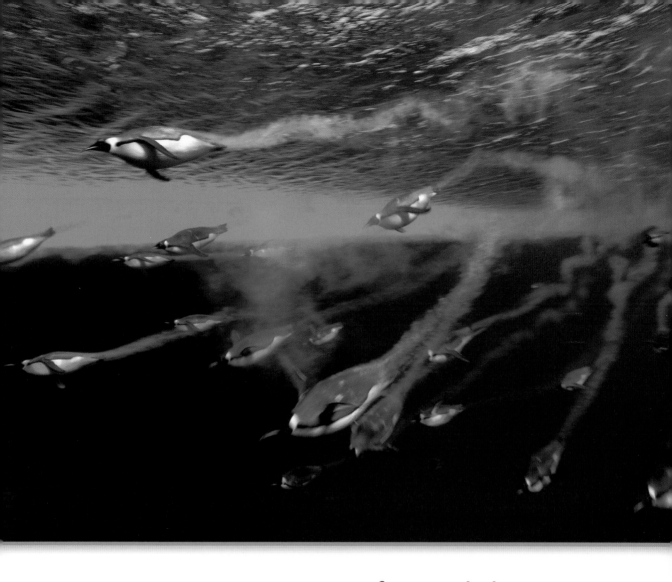

Emperor penguins swim far and dive deep into the ocean to find food.

They dive for food about 26 times every day.

What Hunts Emperor Penguins?

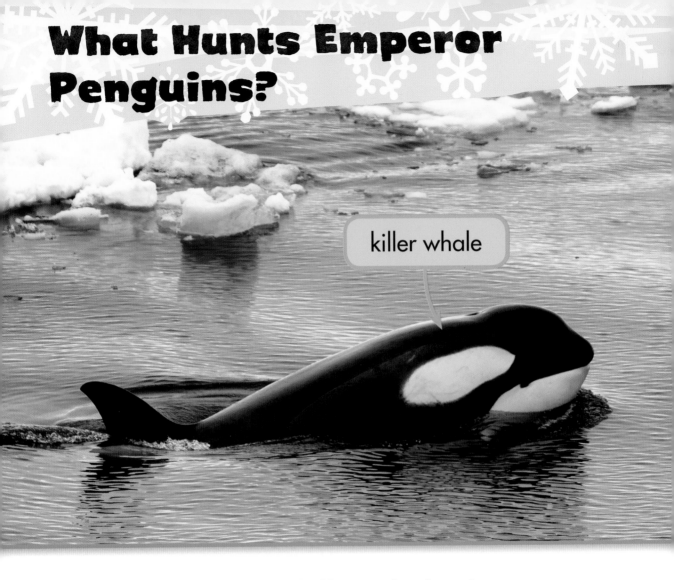

killer whale

Leopard seals and killer whales hunt emperor penguins.

These animals often sneak up on the penguins as they enter the water.

skua

Emperor penguins also have enemies on the ice during daylight hours.

Sea birds like skuas and petrels eat eggs and baby penguins.

Do Emperor Penguins Live in Groups?

Emperor penguins live in groups called colonies.

There can be between a few hundred birds and tens of thousands of birds in a colony.

Emperor penguins travel long distances during the year.

They travel to different places to lay eggs and search for food.

What Do Emperor Penguins Do at Night?

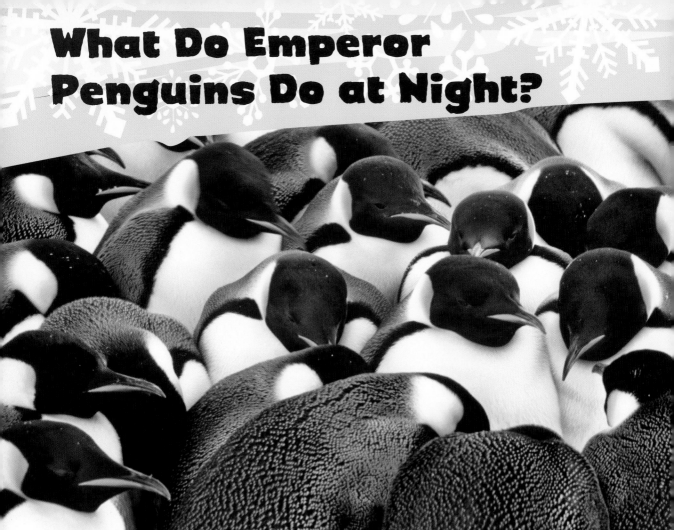

Emperor penguins usually rest more during night-time hours.

They keep warm by huddling together in groups.

Emperor penguins can sleep while they are standing up.

This keeps their bodies away from the cold ice.

What Are Baby Emperor Penguins Like?

egg

A mother emperor penguin lays one egg every year.

The father balances the egg on his feet. He keeps the egg warm until it hatches.

Both parents take turns caring for the fuzzy **chick** for about 150 days.

Then young emperor penguins leave their parents to explore the snowy world around them!

Emperor Penguin Body Map

flipper

beak

feathers

foot

Glossary

 **active** busy doing lots of things

 **Antarctica** very cold continent located at the South Pole

 **chick** baby bird. Baby emperor penguins are called chicks.

 **krill** small shrimp-like animals

 **waterproof** not allowing water to soak through

 **webbed** having toes that are connected by a thin fold of skin

Find Out More

Books

Goldish, Meish. *Emperor Penguin: The World's Biggest Penguin*. New York City: Bearport, 2010.

Miller, Sara. *Emperor Penguins of the Antarctic*. New York City: PowerKids Press, 2009.

Websites

www.kidskonnect.com/subject-index/13-animals/44-penguins.html

Find out interesting facts about penguins on this Website.

www.kids.nationalgeographic.com/kids/animals/creaturefeature/emperor-penguin/

Watch a video on emperor penguins and learn all about them on the National Geographic Website.

Index